DETROIT PUBLIC LIBRARY

P9-CCZ-028

KIDS' FUNNIEST RIDDLES

Charles Keller

... THE BIG QUESTION!..

Illustrated by Jeff Sinclair

CHASE BRANCH LIBRARY
17731 W. SEVEN MILE RD.
DETROIT, MI 48235
578-8002

Sterling Publishing Co., Inc.

New York

JUL   2002

CH

To Gabriel and Bowen

I would like to acknowledge the help of Marcus Bocchino, Rhoda Crispell, and Brenda Gordon.

Library of Congress Cataloging-in-Publication Data

10   9   8   7   6   5   4   3   2   1

First paperback edition published in 2001 by
Sterling Publishing Company, Inc.
387 Park Avenue South, New York, N.Y. 10016
© 2000 by Charles Keller
Distributed in Canada by Sterling Publishing
℅ Canadian Manda Group, One Atlantic Avenue, Suite 105
Toronto, Ontario, Canada M6K 3E7
Distributed in Great Britain and Europe by Chris Lloyd at Orca Book
Services, Stanley House, Fleets Lane, Poole BH15 3AJ, England.
Distributed in Australia by Capricorn Link (Australia) Pty. Ltd.
P.O. Box 704, Windsor, NSW 2756 Australia
Manufactured in the United States of America
All rights reserved

Sterling ISBN 0-8069-1361-4 Trade
              0-8069-1360-6 Paper

Contents

1. Fools Rush In

How did the lumberjack get information from the computer?

He logged on.

Why did the big, ugly monster cross the road?

Are you going to tell him he can't?

Why was the little piece of bread poor?

It didn't have enough dough.

Why was the ghost afraid?

It was spooked.

What do you call a dog with the flu?
A germy shepherd.

What long, slippery fish is like a computer message?
An eel-mail.

What do sea monsters eat?
Submarine sandwiches.

Where do rabbits go to hear singing?
To the hop-era.

What do cows say when they cry?
"Moo-hoo."

Do cows ever play records?
No, they play cowsettes.

What do you get when you cross a dragon with a wheat field?
Burnt toast.

What is the opposite of the Easter Bunny?
The Wester Bunny.

What do you get when you cross a fashion model with a ghost?
A cover ghoul.

Why don't rabbits get hot in the summer?
They have hare conditioning.

What's a ghost's favorite food?
Dreaded wheat.

What happens when you pamper a cow?
You get spoiled milk.

Who do birds marry?
Their tweethearts.

What happened when the chicken got run over crossing the road?
It was flat-henned.

What do you call a group of quiet dogs?
Hush puppies.

Why do birds wear watches?
Because time flies.

Where do Eskimo barbers live?
In wig-loos.

What did the dog need after it swallowed the clock?
A bath. It was full of ticks.

How do you make a shoe stop talking?
You stick your foot in its mouth.

What do you call a skinny bird?
A narrow sparrow.

What mouse won't eat cheese?
A computer mouse.

Where do stockings go for help?
Their support group.

What do you get when you cross binoculars with an oyster?
A see-shell.

What do you get when you cross a huge hairy creature with a couch potato?

The Adominable Slowman.

Where does bread go to mail its letters?

To the toast office.

Why did the computer company go out of business?

It cashed in its chips.

Where does Silly Billy sleep?

In a fool-size bed.

What would you get if you gave sour cream to a monster?

Scream cream.

Where do you put milk for a Martian cat?

In a flying saucer.

Why did the salad bowl crash?

It hit some iceberg lettuce.

What belt do you wear when you're moving?

A seat belt.

What language do birds speak?

Wing-lish.

How did the dog cross the road?

By waggin'.

What's the warmest part of a car?

The muffler.

Why wouldn't the rice stay in the bowl?

It was wild rice.

Why can't you depend on roosters and hens in a battle?

They always chicken out.

Why are bunny slippers so comfortable?

Because they are like walking on hare.

What do you get when you cross a chicken and a guitar?

A chicken that plucks itself.

What do you call a baby in outer space?

An unidentified crying object.

What does a car do when it gets scared?

It runs.

What do you call a clam that doesn't share?

A selfish shellfish.

What's a car's favorite TV game show?

Wheel of fortune.

How do you know when seafood is angry?
The clams are steamed.

Why did the baseball player remain single?
He was always playing the field.

When do baseball players like pantyhose?
When there's a run in them.

What's a waiter's favorite constellation?
The Big Tipper.

Where do baseball catchers sit for dinner?
Behind the plate.

Why did the shellfish go to the doctor?
It felt clammy.

Why did the chicken cross the road?
To boldly go where no chicken has ever gone before.

What kind of fabric do balding men want?
Mo-hair.

Why did the barber think his life was exciting?
It was one close shave after another.

Why were the astronauts dizzy?
They kept seeing stars.

What do you call it when a robot sleeps all winter?
Cybernation.

What did the bed say to the wind?
"Are you looking to blow my cover?"

2. Running Amok

Why did everyone laugh at the cigarette?
  It was the butt of the joke.

What hamburger tells your fortune?
  Medium.

What has wheels, an umbrella, and hates cold canines?
  A hot-dog stand.

What do you call a fire-fighting animal out of uniform?

Smokey the Bare.

What do bugs drink?

Apple spider.

Why was the spider so grumpy in the morning?

Because it woke up on the wrong side of the web.

What do you get when you cross a talkative person with an apple?

A yapple.

Why didn't the worms go on Noah's Ark in apples?

Because they had to go in pears.

What do you get when you cross Superman with Batman?

Blooperman.

What was Batman doing going up a tree?

Looking for Robin's nest.

What did one leaf say to the other?

"Have a nice fall."

What does a spider order for lunch?

A hamburger with flies.

What do you call a flying turtle?
A shellicoptor.

What does a bear wear in her hair?
Bear-ettes.

What do you get when you cross a turtle with a porcupine?
A slow poke.

What's a polar bear's favorite cereal?
Ice Krispies.

What does a troll do when it breaks a toe?
It calls a troll truck.

What starts with T, ends with T, and is full of T?
A teapot.

What happened when the light bulbs went on strike?
A dim outlook was predicted.

Why did Sitting Bull consider changing his name after giving a speech?
He received a standing ovation.

What do you call a watch that doesn't work?
Timeless.

What do you call someone who reads feet instead of palms?

A sole searcher.

Why was the detective sitting on his luggage?

He was on the case.

What happened when the apple and the orange went into business together?

They had a fruitful partnership.

How did the clocks enjoy the party?

They had a great time.

Why did the tree decide to move to another forest?

It wanted to branch out.

What do you call an ill tree?

A sickamore.

Why did Silly Billy carry a clock and a bird on Halloween?

To go tick-or-tweeting.

What do you get when you combine Batman with a big meatball sandwich?

A super hero.

Why didn't the dinosaur cross the road?
They didn't have roads back then.

What kind of dinosaur knew all kinds of words?
A bronthesaurus.

Why do spiders spin webs?
Because they can't spin yarns.

How does a light protect itself from the sun's rays?
By wearing a lampshade.

What happened when the electrician fixed the light socket?
He got a charge out of it.

Why did the candle fall in love?
It met the perfect match.

What group does Macintosh belong to?
The Apple Corps.

Why was the tea bag fired?
It was always getting into hot water.

What happened when the feet had a fight?
They became arch enemies.

What do you put on a foot when he has a cold?
Achoo.

What happened when the turtle stepped on a live wire?

Shell shock.

What koala has no clothes?

A koala bear.

What did the foot say to quiet the shoe?

"Put a sock in it."

Why did the hamburger bun enter the beauty contest?

She wanted to be a roll model.

What do you call a scared dinosaur?
Nervous Rex.

What did the coffee say to its sad friend?
"Perk up."

Why did the dolphin cross the road?
He did it on porpoise.

What do you get when you cross an alligator with a pickle?
A crocodill.

Why did the whale eat two ships loaded with potatoes?
Because no one can eat only one potato ship.

What do you get when you cross a dinosaur with a pig?
Jurassic pork.

How do whales start fires?
They rub two fish sticks together.

Which case did the detective fall asleep on?
The pillowcase.

How does a hot dog wear its hair?
In a bun.

Why did the spider move its home from the window?

It wanted to change web sites.

What is a vampire's favorite sport?
Casketball.

What did the snail say when it went for a ride on the turtle's back?

"Wheee!"

What's really big and makes a loud cracking noise?

A whale trying to use a bathtub.

What do you get when you cross Superman with a main road?

A superhighway.

3. Win Some, Lose Some

What kind of gloves jump up when you count to ten?

Boxing gloves.

Why did the gangster get rid of the pigs?

He didn't like squealers.

Why did the white flakes fall so slowly?

They were in snow motion.

What do you call a snake that drinks too much coffee?

A hyper viper.

What do snowmen ride?

Ice-cycles.

What do you call a monkey whose bananas have been taken away?

Furious George.

How did the hairbrush get rid of the annoying comb?

It gave it the brushoff.

How do you unnerve a serpent?
Rattle snake.

What do you call a glass you can drink from for 60 minutes?
An hourglass.

What primate can fly?
A hot-air baboon.

What's a boxer's favorite part of a joke?
The punch line.

What do you get when a fiery dragon jumps into the sea?
A heat wave.

What boats are awarded to winners?
Championships.

Who helps Bugs Bunny put on his clothes?
His hare dresser.

How did the knife beat the fork home?
It took a shortcut.

What newspaper puts people to sleep?
The Daily Snooze.

What do you call the two owners of a seagoing vessel?
A partnership.

Why was the skindiver angry when the dry cleaner cleaned his suit?
It was a wet suit.

What kind of man has to shave twice a day?
A two-faced man.

Why did the cat snuggle up to the computer?
It was a laptop.

What kind of musical fork doesn't go with a knife?
A tuning fork.

What kind of computer did cavemen use?
A B.C.-P.C.

How did the sugar cane charm the people?
With sweet talk.

What did Silly Billy say when he opened the box of Cheerios?
"Look! Doughnut seeds!"

Why are want ads so hard to find?
They are classified.

What did the disposable razor say when they threw it away?
"That was a close shave."

What bank deals in information not money?
  A data bank.

How did Charlie Brown's dog act like a private eye?
  By Snooping around.

What happened to the used broom?
  It was swept aside.

What's another name for a raincoat?
  A drench coat.

What did the soda glass say to the nervous ice cube?

"Chill out!"

What part of the ship is always tired?

The pooped deck.

Why did the newspaper reporter buy a blanket?

For undercover reporting.

How does corn laugh?

"Schuck, schuck, schuck."

What did the farmer give his girlfriend on Valentine's Day?

Hogs and kisses.

What happens when sugar gets into a fight?

It takes its lumps.

What do you call a pig that isn't honest?

Phony baloney.

What happened when the puzzles had an argument?

Cross words.

Why do they measure snakes in inches?

Because they have no feet.

Why do werewolves buy newspapers?
To check their horroscopes.

Where does a bandleader keep his music?
In a notebook.

What do you get when you cross a zebra with a pig?
Striped sausages.

What happens when corn catches a cold?
It gets an ear ache.

What lottery did the broom win?
The sweepstakes.

What happens when you don't clean your mirror?

It gives you a dirty look.

What do chess players have for breakfast?
Pawncakes.

Why couldn't Mozart find his teacher?
His teacher was Haydn.

What do you call a snowman in June?
A puddle.

What would you get if you crossed a pie with a monkey?

A meringue-utan.

Why was the snowman nervous about getting married?

He had cold feet.

What would you get if Snoopy slept too close to the campfire?

A hot dog.

Why did the orchestra leader cross the road?
To face the music.

What do musicians do during hard times?
They band together.

4. Laughing Stock

Why did the ice cream man give the duck a free cone?

Because he looked a little down.

What has a hundred legs and lives on yogurt?

An aerobics class.

When do playing cards get along well?

When they are two of a kind.

What do ducks use to make their pain go away?
Quackupuncture.

What do you get when you cross sticky candy
and a quacky bird?
Taffy Duck.

Where did the police put the ape when he broke
the law?
Behind monkey bars.

What do cats call their grandfather?
Grandpaw.

What is a frog's favorite flower?
A crocus.

Why did the bartender give himself up to the police?
He felt comfortable behind bars.

What worms live in a king's castle?
Knight crawlers.

What kind of car did Humpty Dumpty drive?
A Yolkswagon.

What is a centipede?
An inchworm that switched to the metric system.

How did the frog win the jumping race?
By leaps and bounds.

Why wouldn't they let the cat use the computer?
It kept chasing the mouse.

Why are cats great racers?
They are good in the long stretch.

What do cats cook when they're in a hurry?
Minute-mice.

How do slugs begin their fairy tales?
"Once upon a slime."

What can't be used until it's broken?
An egg.

What kind of stories do frogs like?
Ones with a hoppy ending.

What did one top say to the other?
"Let's go for a spin."

What part of a hospital is reserved for farm animals?
The chicken wing.

Why didn't the police believe Mother Goose?
She kept telling them fairy tales.

What has to crawl twelve times to go a foot?
An inch worm.

What do you call a mummy that has a job?
A working stiff.

What credit card does Mickey Mouse carry?
Mousetercard.

What credit card did Columbus carry?
A Discover Card.

What kind of vehicle snores?
A sleeping car.

What credit card do witches carry?
American Hexpress.

What did the gasoline say to the car?
"What do you take me for, a fuel?"

What did the baker get when he retired?
A twenty-one bun salute.

What colors do football players hate?
Black and blue.

Why did the gambler make sure the cat had plenty to eat?
He wanted to build up the kitty.

How did the eggs cross the road?
They scrambled.

What kind of advice do you get from a cotton swab?
A Q-tip.

Why was the father centipede sad?
The kids needed new shoes.

How do they get football players clean?
They put them on the scrub team.

What does a steamroller have for dessert?
Low-flat ice cream.

How did the eye doctors' convention turn out?
It was a great spectacle.

What's the favorite dessert in prison?
Jail-O.

What does a frog drink when he's on a diet?
Diet Croak.

What do you get when you cross a fairy with a skunk?
Stinkerbell.

What did the egg say when its show was finished?
"That's all, yolks."

What kind of car does Luke Skywalker drive?
A Toy Yoda.

What is slime's favorite game?
"Slimen Says."

Why did the bacon laugh?
Because the egg had a funny yolk.

What's green, has four legs, and will squash you like a bug if it falls out of a tree?
A pool table.

Why don't mummies go on vacation?
Because they might relax and unwind.

What happened when the two ropes played football?
They tied.

What did the elephant say to the woolly mammoth?
"Wow! Where did you get that stunning fur coat?"

What does one prisoner use to call another prisoner?
A cell phone.

What's twelve, white, and cracks easily?
A dozen eggs.

What kind of ball wears shoes?
A football.

5. Going Along for the Ride

What do you call a saw that falls into the ocean?
A seesaw.

In what part of your phone book are cowards listed?
The Yellow Pages.

What washes up on really small beaches?
Microwaves.

What do you get when you cross a grasshopper with a dinosaur?

Bad yard problems.

What do you get when you cross a Mustang with an elephant?

A sports car with plenty of trunk space.

What do you call a movie about a flower salesman?

"Florist Gump."

Why did Paul Revere take the midnight ride?

Because he missed the 10 p.m. bus.

How do turtles talk to each other?
By shellular phone.

What do you get when you cross a crustacean
with a policeman?
A crabby officer.

How did the telephone propose to his girlfriend?
He gave her a ring.

Who watches young squid?
Babysquidders.

Why did the telephone go to the psychiatrist?
It had a few hangups.

What's the hardest thing about being an octopus?
Washing your hands before dinner.

What kind of horse did the headless horseman
ride?
A nightmare.

What kind of money do ponies use?
Horse cents.

What's the noisiest letter in the alphabet?
"Yell-O."

What do you call a grasshopper's accident?
A miss-hop.

What were the pennies talking about?
*I don't know, but they seemed to be making cents to
me.*

What happened when the retired general became
bank president?
He started giving money orders.

What is it called when two cellular phones
almost run into each other?
A close call.

What would you get if you crossed the seventeenth letter of the alphabet with a pickle?
A Q-cumber.

Who wears a mask and haunts talks shows?
The phantom of the Oprah.

What goes clomp, clomp, clomp, clomp, clomp, clomp, clomp, squish?
An octopus with one shoe off.

What did the horse say after finishing its hay?
"That was the last straw."

How did the comic put makeup on his eyelids?
With a one-liner.

What kind of body never needs clothes?
A body of water.

What TV network broadcasts between England and France?
The English Channel.

Who guards the second letter of the alphabet?
A B-keeper.

What do you call two people chatting?
Doubletalk.

When is a leftover not a leftover?
When it's on the right side.

Why didn't the ventriloquist's partner get a job?
Because he was a dummy.

What kind of container never shuts up?
A chatter box.

What does a preacher use to hold up his pants?
A Bible belt.

Why don't hens do stand-up comedy?
They always lay an egg.

How do small horses wear their hair?
In ponytails.

Why was the radio fired?
It kept giving the boss static.

What do you call an imaginary problem?
An obstacle illusion.

Where do flowers sleep when it rains?
In a water bed.

What do you call an unemployed Santa Claus?
A ho-ho hobo.

Why did God create Eve from the ribs of man?
He wanted to split the Adam.

What do you say to a boomerang on its birthday?

"Many happy returns."

What do police officers buy at the bakery?

Copcakes.

What kind of flowers grow under artificial light?

Ultra-violets.

What do tired spices ask for in sports?

Thyme outs.

What did the gingerbread man find on his bed?

A cookie sheet.

What would you get if you crossed a parrot with a caterpillar?

A chatterpillar.

Why did the angel lose its job?

It had harp failure.

What do you give a man who has everything?

Antibiotics.

Why couldn't the moon eat anything more?

It was full.

What do termites do when they want to take a rest?

They take a coffee-table break.

What did the VCR say to the CD player?

"You just don't get the picture, do you?"

What branch of the military flies silly planes?

The Air Farce.

How did the soldier feel about the marksmanship test?

He took a shot at it.

What kind of deal does a dog hate?

A flea bargain.

Why did the bar of soap confess?
  It wanted to come clean.

Why was Tweety Bird the first one to go to the hair stylist?
  Because the early bird gets the perm.

How did the Easter Bunny get to work?
  Rabbit Transit.

Why did the duck cross the road?
  He wanted to fix a quack in the cement.

What do you call a cricket that says one thing and does another?
  A hypocricket.

How do billboards talk?
Sign language.

Why did the fireplace call the doctor?
Because the chimney had the flu.

Do robots have brothers?
No, they have transistors.

What did the bee say to the flower?
"What time do you open?"

6. Monkeying Around

What did one dish say to the other?
  "Lunch is on me."

What do you call a carousel without brakes?
  A merry-go-round and round and round and round and....

What did Billy say after he learned to count money?

"It all makes cents now."

What is stucco?

What you get when you sit on gummo.

What's the best way to get around on the ocean floor?

By taxi crab.

What does Scrooge wear to play ice hockey?

Cheap skates.

Why couldn't the girl climb the short tree?

Its bark was worse than its height.

Why did the elephant want to buy a bigger car?

It needed more trunk space.

Why didn't Mrs. Skeleton leave Mr. Skeleton?

She didn't have the heart.

What is dark but made by light?

Your shadow.

What do you get when you cross a rabbit with a spider?

A hare net.

Why did the golf ball get mad at the golf club?
It was teed off.

What did one golfer say to the other?
"May the course be with you."

How do you get rid of a track star?
Give him the runaround.

Where do books sleep?
Under their covers.

How do shepherds call to their lost sheep?
"Where are ewe?"

What kind of food is hard to catch?
Fast food.

What meal helps drivers avoid accidents?
Brake fast.

What did the mama rabbit say to the babies?
"Some bunny loves you."

What do rich rabbits eat?
Carats.

What do you give four weathermen when they go fishing?
A four-cast.

What kind of tales do dwarfs tell?
Short stories.

Where do you take a crybaby grape?
To the winery.

What kind of streets do skeletons like?
Dead ends.

Why did the woman refuse to marry the invisible man?
She didn't see anything in him.

How does a dog stop a VCR?
It presses the paws button.

What do you call a cold puppy sitting on a rabbit?
A chili dog on a bunny.

If a skyscraper could talk, what would it tell you?
A tall story.

What do you call a script for a horror movie?
A screamplay.

How do dogs go camping?
They ruff it.

How did the bush ignore the weather?
It scrubbed it off.

Why did the computer go to the hospital?
It had a slipped disk.

Why do they carve pumpkins at Halloween?
Did you ever try to carve a grape?

Who do monsters buy their cookies from?
The Ghoul Scouts.

What kind of sauce do sheep use at their cookout?
Baa-baa-cue sauce.

Why is a dog so hot in summer?
Because it wears a coat and pants.

What did the baby computer say to its mother?
"I want my data."

Why did the skeleton join the motorcycle gang?
It was bone to be wild.

Why don't monsters attack people in cars?
They don't like canned food.

Why did Silly Billy put running shoes on his head?
So he could jog his memory.

What do you call a queen that plays golf?
The Queen of Clubs.

What did the computer do in Hawaii?
Surf the Net.

What would you get if you crossed an elephant with an alligator?
An elephator.

What did one hill say to the other after the earthquake?
"It wasn't my fault."

Who is the smartest monster?
Frank Einstein.

Why did the germ cross the microscope?
To get to the other slide.

What did the big grape say to the little grape on Christmas?
"'Tis the season to be jelly."

Why did the shy pebble cry?
It wished it was a little boulder.

What did the hole say to the golf ball?
"Why don't you drop in sometime?"

Why can't skeletons play music in church?
They have no organs.

Where does a roadrunner go when it's hungry?
To a fast-food restaurant.

What do you get when you cross a kangaroo and a sheep?
A sweater with big pockets.

What's a turtle's least favorite food?
Fast food.

What do Scandinavians have to do to complete a marathon?
Pass the Finnish line.

How does a drink made from grapes complain?
It whines.

What happens when a baby falls?
Baby boom.

7. Smart Cookies

How do bowling pins make demands?
They go on strike.

What did the bowler roll toward his car?
A spare.

Why did the hurried bowler want to roll a strike?
He had no time to spare.

What was the basketball player doing at breakfast?
Dunking donuts.

How do you get Lyme disease on the moon?
From luna ticks.

What's red, yellow, and very messy?
A fire truck stuck in a pool of mustard.

Why did the retired basketball player become a judge?
So he could stay on the court.

What squawks and jumps out of airplanes?
A parrot-trooper.

Why did the shepherd chase after the fugitive?
He was on the lamb.

What would you get if you cross a nectarine with a giraffe?
A peach with a reach.

What kind of house has no experience?
A greenhouse.

Why did the palm tree cross the road?
It had a date.

Was the pretzel upset?
Yes, it was bent out of shape.

What kind of tree doesn't like bare feet?
A shoe tree.

Who brings presents to lobsters?
Sandy Claws.

Where did the tree keep its luggage?
In its trunk.

What did the mouse send over the Internet?
Eek-mail.

How did the man get rid of his shoes?
He gave them the boot.

What did the basketball player ask for from his fairy godmother?
Three swishes.

What did the toast say when it was left in the toaster too long?
"This really burns me up!"

Why wasn't the computer's high-wire act a success?
It worked without the Net.

What do you get when you cross a chicken with a bicycle?
A hen-speed bike.

What kind of mail do convict workers in gangs receive?
Chain letters.

What did the baby chick say when it couldn't get out of its shell?

"You got me into this, now get me out!"

Why did the poppy seed cross the road?

It was on a roll.

What are people doing when they argue about their inheritances?

Splitting heirs.

What do clams and oysters do over the holidays?

Shellebrate.

Why did the tree get lost in the woods?
It took the wrong root.

What do you get when you cross a praying
mantis with a termite?
A big thing that says grace before eating your house.

What happened when the monster ate the
electric company?
It was in shock for a week.

Why is the dinosaur healthier than the dragon?
Because a dinosaur doesn't smoke.

What do you get when you cross Frankenstein with a pig?

Frankenswine.

What kind of weed grows in a taxi?

Cab grass.

What kind of car does an electrician drive?

A Voltswagen.

From what kind of dish does a car eat?

A license plate.

How did the gnat send the ant a computer message?

By flea-mail.

Why did the basketball coach flood the gym?

He wanted his team to sink some baskets.

Why did Washington cross the Delaware?

Because the chicken needed a ride.

What did the detective say when he finished packing his suitcase?

"Case closed."

What animal talks too much?

A yak.

Where does a shoe salesman go for vacation?
Boot camp.

What do criminals sleep on?
Rap sheets.

What did one flower say to the other at the break of day?
"Morning, Bud."

Why did the turkey cross the road?
The chicken retired and moved to Florida.

Where does Amtrak send its new conductors?
Training school.

Why was everyone on the pirate ship afraid of the barber?
He was a cutthroat.

Why was the Marine discharged from the service?
He was rotten to the Corps.

What did the luggage say at the airport?
"Carry on."

Why wouldn't the pig let the other animals pass him?
He was a road hog.

Why was the bull's credit card canceled?
He wouldn't stop charging.

Why did the investor buy shares in the comedy club.
He wanted a laughing stock.

Why did the Dalmatian go to the dry cleaners?
Its coat had spots all over it.

What did the cat say when it wanted to go out?
"Me-out."

How did the fisherman create problems?

He opened a can of worms.

What do you get from a vampire at the North Pole.

Frost bite.

Why did the cook try to make the cucumber laugh?

To see if it was picklish.

How do you fool a sheep?

You pull the wool over its eyes.

8. Batten Down the Hatches

What is a fish's favorite book?
The Adventures of Huck Fin.

What insect breathes fire?
A dragonfly.

What happened to the bedbug who fell in love?
It got married in the spring.

How do fleas travel?
They itch hike.

What would you get if you crossed a tiger with a Japanese restaurant?
A man-eating sushi.

Who grants fishes wishes?
The fairy codmother.

What did the duck say when she bought lipstick?
"Just put it on my bill."

What's a ghost's favorite direction?
Horror-zontal.

What kind of town has a laundry service for sheets?

A ghost town.

Why was Jesse James's brother so outspoken?
Because he was Frank.

What kind of gum did Al Capone chew?
Machine gum.

How do tigers like campers?
Raw.

Why is a rock band so mean?
They beat the drums and pick on the guitar.

What did the leopard say in the cafeteria?
"Save me a spot."

Why did the ghost cross the road?
Because the spirit moved him.

How does a bird go to church?
On a wing and a prayer.

What do you call a cow that doesn't give milk?
A milk dud.

Why was the calendar jumping?
It was the leap year.

Why did the clock hang around the park all day?

It had time on its hands.

Why did the baseball player cross the road?

He was trying to get home.

Why did the baseball player cross the road?

It was a shortstop.

Where do you go if you want more land for your house?

To a yard sale.

What bird spies on other birds in the forest?
A woodpeeper.

What's the best way to transport a bunch of cattle?
Hire a moo-ving van.

Where do bugs buy their groceries?
The flea market.

What do potatoes bet with?
Chips.

What do you say when you see low-flying birds?
"Duck!"

What happens when you annoy a black bird?
It goes stark raven mad.

Why did the baseball players have to stay at a hotel?
They were thrown out at home.

Why didn't the rock have any feelings?
It had a heart of stone.

What kind of donuts can't pass a school test?
Flunkin' donuts.

What do you call a boring bird?
A dull gull.

Who stole the soap?
The robber ducky.

What did the big hand on the clock say to the little hand?
"I'll be back in an hour."

What did the wind say to the ghost?
"Just passing through."

Where can you fall without getting hurt?
Asleep.

What should you do if someone is out to steal your Rolex?
Watch it.

How much sleep does an eyelid need?
About forty winks.

What does glue have with coffee?
Pastries.

Would you believe a person who talks in his sleep?
No, because he's lying.

What did the umpire yell when the baseball hit the chicken?
"Fowl ball."

What crawls, has scales, and lives in Emerald City?

The lizard of Oz.

What do you get when you cross a mummy with a CD?

A wrap song.

What do astronauts eat for breakfast?

Flying sausages.

What did the tailor say to the customer?

"Suit yourself."

Why did the rodent quit the relay team?
  It didn't want to become part of the rat race.

Why did the car stop in the middle of the road?
  It was wheelie, wheelie tired.

9. Hanging In There

When is an arm dangerous?
When it's a firearm.

Why don't buildings like news reports?
They have their own stories.

What do you get when you cross a superstar with a public official?
Someone superficial.

What do you get when you mix together a lighthouse, a rose trellis and a strong windstorm?

A beacon, lattice, and tornado sandwich.

What's the difference between an onion and an accordion?

No one cries when you cut up an accordion.

Why did the turkey cross the road?

To get to Mexico where they don't celebrate Thanksgiving.

Why do they call a queen's wand a scepter?

Because everyone works scepter.

Which one of King Arthur's knights danced the most?

Sir Dancelot.

What kind of fish likes to duel?

A swordfish.

What restaurant did Adam and Eve eat in?

The Garden of Eating.

Where do lawyers aspire to play tennis?

At the Supreme Court.

What do you call an elderly herb specialist?

An old thymer.

Why is the rain considered clumsy?
It's always falling.

How can you make sure no one will take your pendant?
Locket.

Why do deer use discount coupons?
They like to save big bucks and lots of doe.

How do poets take their wedding vows?
For better or verse.

Why was Count Dracula fired?
He made a few grave errors.

Where do old bicycle tires go?
To the old spokes' home.

Why couldn't the window shade see?
It was a blind.

Why did the president go to a furniture store?
To get a new cabinet.

Why did the policeman put handcuffs on the front door of a home?
He was making a house arrest.

How did the contest between two ropes turn out?
The score was tied up.

Was the table shy?
Yes, it was reserved.

What do you call a failed pelican?
A pelican't.

Was the turtle-and-rabbit race close?
Yes, it was won by a hare.

What roads are always angry?
Crossroads.

What part of the house enjoys bad weather?
Storm windows.

What's black and white and lives in Hawaii?
A lost penguin.

What happened when the dictionary got angry?
No one could get a word out of it.

What do they call young plants in Belgium?
Brussels sprouts.

Where did they send the ink that was found
guilty of forgery?
To the state pen.

What's a jockey's favorite vegetable?
Horseradish.

Why was Rudolph wet?
Because of the rain deer.

What kind of sweater does a traffic policeman wear?
A pullover.

What do you get when you cross a rabbit with a spider web?
A hare net.

Why did the vampire run out of the restaurant?
Because he heard someone order a stake.

How do you buy a thundercloud?
With a rain check.

When is an extra tire most popular?
In its spare time.

Are deer good sports?
Sure, they're game.

What should you do if a female journalist steals?
Reporter.

What's a psychic's favorite sport?
Crystal ball.

Who likes to eat at underwater restaurants?
Scuba diners.

What did the determined Hawaiian farmer say?
"If I can't grow corn, I'll raise cane."

What car breathes fire?
A station dragon.

Who yelled "The British are coming!"
backwards?
Paul Reverse.

What private eye stepped on chewy candy?
A gumshoe.

What did the boy say to the insect?
  "Bug off."

What did the Titanic say before the crash?
  "I have a sinking feeling about that iceberg."

Why did the baby chicks cross the road?
  They were egged on.

What do you get if you cross a magician and a secret agent?
  James Wand.

How did the golfer waste time?
  By puttering around.

Why was the criminal afraid to talk in front of the beekeeper?

He was wearing a bug.

What do you get when you cross a clumsy insect and a grasshopper?

A clodhopper.

What do lamps think up?

Bright ideas.

What do you call a smart snowfall?

A brainstorm.

Who was Robin Hood's favorite cook?

Fryer Tuck

What kind of journey can you take without leaving your home?

An ego trip.

What has 18 legs, catches flies, and has red spots?

A baseball team with the measles.

What would you get if you crossed a newt and a poodle?

A newdle.

What did the parrot say when it wanted a frog?

"Polly wants a croaker."

What do you call a broken record?
A smash hit.

What does a parakeet say when it's hungry?
"Long time no seed."

What's green and smells like paint?
Green paint.

10. In a Nutshell

How did the sick lamb get to the hospital?
By lambulance.

Why didn't the lamb make a sound all day?
It didn't like to bleat between meals.

Who takes care of little goats?
Their nanny.

What did the chocolate drink say to get the soda's attention?
"Yoo-Hoo!"

What soft drinks do squirrels like?
Oaka-Cola.

What was the broken soda machine out of?
Order.

What does an Egyptian doorbell say?
"Toot and come in."

What did one fireplace say to the other?
"I've got hearth burn."

When does a day begin sadly?
When it's in mourning.

What do bees say on warm days?
"Swarm, isn't it?"

What does the sun drink out of?
Sunglasses.

What kind of witch turns out the lights?
A lights-witch.

How many witches does it take to change a light bulb?
Only one, but it turns it into a toad.

What did one zombie say to the other?
"Get a life!"

What does a train conductor say when all his passengers look tired and lifeless?
"All are bored."

What street do lions hang out on?
Mane Street.

What has no hair and thinks it's the national dog of the United States?
The bald beagle.

What jungle animal is always pouting?
A whinoceros.

Why did the fisherman go to the doctor?
He lost his herring.

What do you call a piano that hasn't been used in a long time?
Key-bored.

What's a plumber's favorite song?
"Singing in the Drain."

Why did the fisherman use a microphone?
He was sportscasting.

Why shouldn't you insult a group of lions?
You might hurt their pride.

What kind of animal puts other creatures in a trance?
A hypnopotamus.

Why did the bird wear a toupee?
It was a bald eagle.

Where do risk-taking hockey players skate?
On thin ice.

How did the hockey player become friends with the swimmer?
By breaking the ice.

Why was the fruit locked up?
It went bananas.

How does a musician choose his guitar?
He takes his pick.

What do you call a lazy baby kangaroo?
A pouch potato.

Why did the celery cross the road?
It was stalked.

How do you fix a broken pumpkin?
With a pumpkin patch.

Why did the friendly cowboy prefer riding
bareback?

He didn't want to stirrup trouble.

Where do owls stay when they go on trips?

At a hoot-el.

What do cowboys wear when they go to work?

Ranch dressing.

Why was the plumber fired?

He kept getting into hot water.

How does a skunk call home?
On a smellular phone.

Why did the strawberry cross the road?
To get out of a jam.

What do you call a hat on roller skates?
A roller derby.

What do you call a truck with indigestion?
A hiccup truck.

What do you call a hippo that never stops eating?
A hippobottomless.

How do you find a missing train?
Follow its tracks.

Which two mountains are opposites?
Mount Everest and Mount Rushmore.

Why do airplane pilots always fly past Peter Pan's island?
Because the sign says "Never Never Land."

What's black and white and wet all over?
A zebra taking a shower.

Do people like to vacation at the beach?
Shore.

Why are models good accountants?

Because they're good with figures.

What kind of footwear does someone with a sore throat wear?

Hoarse shoes.

What do ants sing before the start of a ball game?

The National Ant-them.

What did the rabbit say when the doorbell rang?

"Will some bunny answer the door?"

What do gymnasts use to spice up their food in July?

Summer salt.

What cable channel should insomniacs watch?

The all-snooze network.

What did the cow say when the farmer sold the milk?

"Show me the moo-lah."

What do you get if you cross a rainstorm and a convertible?

A carpool.

What do you call a cow that steers a car?

A cattle drive.

What did they do when the canoe misbehaved?

They paddled it.

About the Author

Charles Keller has been working and playing with comedy all his life. Working for CBS as a script consultant, he edited many of the great classic sitcoms, such as *M*A*S*H, All in the Family,* and *The Mary Tyler Moore Show,* and he also worked on other prime-time comedy shows. He got started writing children's books because he didn't like many of the ones he read and thought he could do better. Now, over 50 books later, he maintains the country's largest archive of children's rhymes, riddles, witty sayings, and jokes, and he constantly updates his massive collection. When he isn't writing children's books, he can be found creating educational software for children. Born in New York, Charles Keller is a graduate of St. Peter's College. He presently resides in Union City, New Jersey.

About the Illustrator

Jeff Sinclair has been drawing cartoons ever since he could hold a pen. He has won several local and national awards for cartooning and humorous illustration. When he is not at his drawing board, he can be found renovating his house and working on a water garden in the backyard. Jeff lives in Vancouver, British Columbia, Canada, with his wife, Karen, son, Brennan, daughter, Conner, and golden Lab, Molly.

Index